Old SAN JUAN
El Morro
San Cristóbal

🌸 AMERICAN & WORLD GEOGRAPHIC PUBLISHING

Published in cooperation with the Eastern National Park & Monument Association.

Eastern 🌰 National

San Cristóbal, El Morro and La Fortaleza have been designated as World Heritage Sites by UNESCO.

UNESCO

Fort San Cristóbal and Fort El Morro are part of the San Juan National Historic Site administered by the National Park Service Department of the Interior.

Write for our catalog:
American & World Geographic Publishing,
P.O. Box 5630, Helena, MT 59604, or call
1-800-654-1105

Printed in the U.S.A.

Above: Castillo de San Felipe del Morro from the air.
Castillo de San Felipe del Morro desde el aire.

Front cover: La Fortaleza and old city wall.
La Fortaleza y un segmento de las murallas.

Back cover (top): North fortification of San Cristóbal.
Las murallas nortes de San Cristóbal.

Back cover (bottom): Main plaza in El Morro.
La plaza principal de El Morro.

Title page: The flags waving in the wind are the Cross of Burgundy, which was the flag of the Spanish Military units from the 1500s to the 1780s, the flag of Puerto Rico and the flag of the United States.
Las banderas son la Cruz de Borgoña (bandera militar española desde el siglo XVI hasta la década de 1780), la bandera de Puerto Rico, y la bandera de Estados Unidos.

Left: Caballero section of San Cristóbal.
Sección Caballero de San Cristóbal.

Below: Casa Blanca. For more than 250 years, Ponce de León's family lived in this house.
Casa Blanca. Durante más de 250 años fue la residencia de la familia Ponce de León.

FOREWORD

Delightful, lively and a great place to stay awhile…these are my feelings for Old San Juan, Puerto Rico. I really like this place. The sense of history is extremely appealing. After all, La Fortaleza and forts El Morro and San Cristóbal are World Heritage as well as national historic sites. The UNESCO World Heritage Site designation is no small acclaim. It means the world community has deemed these locations an important legacy for all mankind.

Then there are the very warm people with their real sense of community and pride. We strangers were invited into their homes, lives and celebrations.

History blends in well with the color and life of the city. An aqua tropical sea washes its north shore, the imposing remains of the city wall and the beautiful Paseo de la Princesa touch the bay of San Juan on the south. Small and compact, Old San Juan is one of the world's great treasures.

I thank the people of San Juan for allowing us the privilege of presenting this book on their special corner of Puerto Rico. And many thanks to Chesley Moroz and Carmelo Martinez of Eastern National Park & Monument Association for believing in this project, the Puerto Rico Tourism Company, the National Park Service, the folks at the Casa San José and Galería San Juan and all the others who assisted us.

Rick Graetz
American & World Geographic Publishing

Above: Caleta de San Juan in Old San Juan.
Caleta de San Juan en el Viejo San Juan.

PRÓLOGO

Encantador, lleno de vida, un sitio agradable donde pasar un rato...así me parece el Viejo San Juan. ¡Me encanta este lugar! Me atrae su sentido de historia. La Fortaleza y los fuertes de El Morro y San Cristóbal han sido designados Patrimonio Mundial, además de ser sitios históricos nacionales. El nombramiento por UNESCO de San Juan como Patrimonio Mundial significa que la comunidad mundial considera estos lugares el legado de todos los pueblos del mundo.

Aquí viven los puertorriqueños, tan hospitalarios, con un gran sentido de comunidad y orgullo. Nosotros, los extraños, hemos sido invitados a sus hogares, sus vidas y sus fiestas.

La historia se entrelaza con los colores y la vida diaria de la ciudad: el mar azul tropical por el norte, las imponentes murallas de la ciudad y el precioso Paseo de la Princesa al lado de la bahía. Pequeño y compacto, el Viejo San Juan es uno de los grandes tesoros del mundo.

Agradezco a la gente de San Juan el habernos concedido el privilegio de presentar este libro sobre su rincón especial de Puerto Rico. Y muchas gracias a Chesley Moroz y Carmelo Martínez de Eastern National Parks & Monument Association por creer en este proyecto, a la Compañía de Turismo, al Servicio Nacional de Parques, a la gente de la Casa San José y Galería San Juan y a todos los que nos dieron la mano.

Rick Graetz

Above: Plaza de Colón. The statue of Christopher Columbus was erected in 1892.
Plaza de Colón. La estatua de Colón se erigió en 1892.

Top: Fortifications of El Morro and Del Carmen sentry box.
Fortificaciones de El Morro y la garita Del Carmen.

Wandering through the streets of Old San Juan, one can almost hear the sounds of the past: clanking muskets and swords as soldiers march to their posts; their murmured protests against the heat and humidity; moans of prisoners, captured and closed away from the blue Caribbean sky in damp, dark dungeons. One can also sense the hustle and bustle of the marketplace, as it comes to life in the early dawn; noisy vendors hawking their wares, lumbering up the narrow streets with carts and baskets. One can almost smell the stench of animals, the sweat of laborers building the city and paving its streets, and the welcome aroma of strong coffee coming from an open window. Meandering through winding San Sebastian Street, looking down at glazed blue bricks which have paved the streets for over 150 years, one can spot green moss poking up through the cracks. To walk around Old San Juan is to listen to the sounds of the past— they mingle with those of the present.

San Juan is a living city. Alive with myriad sounds, smells, tastes, textures, and even emotions, it is one of the historical treasures of the New World.

Puerto Rico was "discovered" by Christopher Columbus, accompanied by young conquistador Juan Ponce de León in 1493 on his second voyage to the New World. Living on the island were the peaceful Taíno Indians, Arawaks who had migrated centuries before from South America. Their society was agricultural, and their principal encounters with violence and warfare had been with fierce Carib Indians who traveled through the islands massacring and eating their captured

Above: San Justo Street.
Calle de San Justo.

Top: A colorful business sign in Old San Juan.
Un letrero de negocio en el Viejo San Juan.

San Juan Cathedral reflection in windows of a house on San José street.
Reflejo de la Catedral de San Juan en las ventanas de una casa en la Calle de San José.

Caminando por las calles del Viejo San Juan uno casi oye los sonidos del pasado: el tantarantán de los soldados con sus tambores, espadas y mosquetes en sus cambios de guardia, murmurando sus quejas sobre el calor y la humedad; los gemidos de los presos, encerrados muy lejos del cielo azul caribeño; el bullicio del mercado al amanecer con los pregoneros que suben por las calles con sus caballos y canastas; casi se huele el sudor de los peones ocupados en la construcción de la ciudad y la pavimentación de sus calles y el rico aroma del café acabado de colar. Al bajar por la Calle San Sebastián, uno se fija en los adoquines azules y el musgo que se asoma entre ellos ¡llevan 150 años puestos! Caminar por el Viejo San Juan es escuchar los sonidos del pasado y los de hoy.

San Juan es una ciudad viviente. Sus sonidos, aromas, gustos y texturas lo convierten en uno de los tesoros del Nuevo Mundo.

Puerto Rico fue "descubierto" en 1493 por Cristóbal Colón, acompañado de el joven Juan Ponce de León, en su segundo viaje. Los indígenas, los taínos, eran un pueblo agrícola pacífico, araucanos que habían emigrado siglos antes de América del Sur. Sus experiencia con la guerra se limitaba a sus encuentros con los feroces caribes, quienes se paseaban por las islas canibalizando a sus víctimas.

foe. Although Europeans did not war against the Taínos, they exploited them by forcing them into hard labor mining the little gold on the island, and it was not long before these humble people died off.

Fifteen years later the Spanish monarchy decided that Puerto Rico was to become not only a base to fight and conquer the Carib Indians, but also a colony guarding the seafaring gateway to the Americas. Ponce de León was named first governor of the island. He organized an expedition from Hispaniola inland, settling at what is now Caparra. It was, at the time, an extremely uncomfortable settlement, surrounded by swamps full of mosquitoes, and very hard to defend.

Several years later the settlers moved to the small islet we now know as San Juan. Only three-and-one-half miles long and approximately one mile wide, San Juan, with its fine natural harbor in an inlet easily arrived at by sea, was a perfect place to defend. Jagged, steep terrain bordered the entrance to the bay. To the north and east, the Atlantic crashed treacherously over coral reefs, spewing up salt water foam and mist, the inevitable *salitre* that permeates the air of Old San Juan.

San Juan was built quickly and it consisted of, first and foremost, the church, surrounded by 80 houses. These primitive structures were built of wood and covered with thatched straw. The first four main streets were designed in a simple grid system: Calle del Cristo, West Recinto, Caleta San Juan, and Caleta Las Monjas. In a sense, the city looked like an amphitheater, with everything fanning out from the church.

Above: The Old Casino of Puerto Rico built in 1918.
El Casino Viejo de Puerto Rico construído en el 1918.

Facing page (bottom): Looking across Norzagaray Street to the Atlantic Ocean.
Mirando desde la Calle Norzagaray hacia el Atlántico.

Aunque los europeos no guerreaban contra los taínos, los explotaban, obligándolos a los trabajos forzados en las minas del escaso oro de la isla y en poco tiempo los taínos se fueron extinguiendo.

Quince años después la monarquía española decidió que Puerto Rico no solo sería un punto de partida para conquistar a los caribes, sino la Llave de las Indias, guardián de las rutas comerciales.

Juan Ponce de León fue nombrado primer gobernador de la isla. Primero estableció la capital en Caparra pero le resultó muy incómodo por los mosquitos y por ser bastante difícil de defender.

Unos años después se mudó la capital a la isleta que hoy conocemos como el Viejo San Juan. Con sus tres millas y media de largo y una milla de ancho, San Juan gozaba de ciertas ventajas:

The first church of San Juan was built where today's Cathedral of San Juan stands. Originally made of wood and straw, it suffered from tropical storms and fire. It was rebuilt several times, until finally, after much perseverance from the priest, Father Bastides, money and materials were given for a permanent structure. Made of stone, it was a dark and quiet place, with narrow windows and only one door.

The church was built on the most prominent spot of the town, facing the seaport. Ships entering the harbor stopped there for crews to greet local dignitaries and to walk a few steps to the church to give thanks upon having arrived; those leaving, to pray for a safe journey.

Among the first buildings to be built were La Casa Blanca, which housed the Governor's family, the Bishop's house—which, of course, housed the dignitaries of the Spanish Catholic Church—and the Municipal council.

Life in the 16th and 17th centuries was governed by the church and the sword, and the early settlement of San Juan is testimony to that. It became a town of churches and fortifications, and most work was done on building the two.

Governor Juan Ponce de León soon left the island in search of the continent to the north, which he named La Florida. After his death, his family moved to Puerto Rico and resided at Casa Blanca.

One day after a storm a descendent, Doña Isabel Ponce de León, noticed a box floating in

Stormy seas roll toward Old San Juan.

Tormenta en el mar.

su puerto natural de bahía tranquila y entrada por el Atlántico lo hacían un lugar idóneo para defender. El fuerte oleaje del traicionero océano revuelca el salitre, ese aire salado que se siente en toda la ciudad.

San Juan se construyó rápidamente. Primero se levantó la iglesia, hoy la Catedral de San Juan, rodeada de unas 80 casitas, hechas de madera y paja tejida. Las primeras calles fueron la Calle del Cristo, Recinto Oeste, Caleta de San Juan y Caleta de Las Monjas.

La primera iglesia de San Juan se construyó donde hoy en día se levanta la Catedral de San Juan. La iglesia de madera y paja sufrió los embates de las tormentas y los incendios y se reconstruyó varias veces hasta que por fin se construyó de piedra. La iglesia se ubicó en el punto más sobresaliente del poblado, frente al puerto. Las naves que llegaban se detenían para que los tripulantes subieran hasta la iglesia para dar gracias a Dios.

Entre los primeros edificios se construyeron la Casa Blanca, residencia de la familia del gobernador, el Obispado y el Cabildo municipal.

La vida de los siglos XVI y XVII se regía por la iglesia y la espada. San Juan, con sus iglesias y fortificaciones, ejemplarizaba esta vida.

El primer Gobernador, Juan Ponce de León, partió desde Puerto Rico hacia el norte al continente que llamó La Florida. Después de su muerte su familia se quedó en Puerto Rico en la Casa Blanca.

Un buen día, después de una tormenta, una

the bay. Inside was a crucifix which she kept in her home until the remains of her father were brought back to the island and placed in a marble tomb in the Cathedral. For many years afterward, during times of drought, the residents of San Juan took *El Cristo de los Ponce* (the Ponce's Christ), the oldest sculpture in the city, in a religious procession through the streets. Because it had come to them floating on the waters it became a symbol for rain.

When the capital of Puerto Rico was moved from Caparra to San Juan, the pressure to explore and conquer the island and neighboring islands had begun to slow down. Although Puerto Rico did not provide the gold that the Spaniards had anticipated, it was regarded, because of its geographical position, as the gateway to the Greater and Lesser Antilles and the Southern Continent. A frontier against the islands ruled by the feared cannibals, it later became an important bastion against invasion.

San Juan continued to develop. In the very beginning it consisted of a few unpaved streets. It was populated by clergy, the military, and a few Spanish colonizers (and their families) lured by the promise of gold. However, the little ore that existed was soon depleted, and Puerto Rico was seen as one of the poorest colonies. Many wanted to leave the islands for other countries in the New World, but the penalties were severe.

After the church and a home for the bishop,

Top: Statue of St. John the Baptist, the patron saint of the City of San Juan.
Estatua de San Juan Bautista, el santo patrón de la ciudad.

From the top of the Banco Popular building in Old San Juan looking east toward the new city and San Juan Bay.
Desde la azotea del Banco Popular en el Viejo San Juan, mirando hacia el este, el área metropolitana y la bahía de San Juan.

de las descendientes de Ponce de León, doña Isabel, vio una caja flotando en la bahía. La mandó a buscar y dentro encontró un crucifijo. Llamado el Cristo de los Ponce, se le pedía lluvia en tiempo de sequía, ya que había llegado por el agua.

Cuando se mudó la capital de Caparra a San Juan, el apremio por explorar y conquistar la isla y las islas cercanas comenzaba a disminuir. Aunque Puerto Rico no había producido el oro que los españoles habían previsto, se le consideraba por su ubicación "la Llave de las Indias." Era una frontera contra los temidos caníbales y se convirtió en un importante bastión.

San Juan seguía creciendo. Al principio había un par de calles pobladas por religiosos, militares y uno que otro colonizador atraído por la esperanza de encontrar oro. Al quedarse la isla sin oro se consideraba que ya no tenía riquezas que ofrecer;

a fortress-home of stone and tamped earth was built for the governor and his family. Then, a government headquarters, followed by barracks for the militia, homes for governing settlers, then residences, however humble, for the people who provided services to the settlers.

But the complex still was not strong enough to ward off the French corsairs or English pirates. These buccaneers seized not only many vessels en route to Europe loaded with treasures and commodities but also inbound ships loaded with Spanish supplies and merchandise.

The first component of the defense system was La Fortaleza. Built mainly for protection against the Carib Indians, it looked more like a medieval castle than an actual fort. Because it was built not at the harbor entrance but inside, on the bay, enemies approaching from the north thought the town was unprotected, and San Juan became easy prey. La Fortaleza, many complained, should have been built on *el morro*, the headland or knoll which towered over the entrance to the port. In 1539, building on San Felipe del Morro to augment La Fortaleza finally began, albeit slowly.

In the next decades French and English pirates forced the Spanish empire to fortify its harbors in earnest. By the time Sir Francis Drake assaulted the fort, in 1595, it had 32 cannon. After a fierce battle and a loss of many lives, he was thwarted. Three years later, however, the Earl of Cumberland conquered San Juan by land. Six weeks after he took El Morro, an outbreak of dysentery killed so many of his troops that he gave up his prize and sailed away. Spanish forces reconquered the territory, and decided that the entire city should

Above: Sunset along the curve of the bay in Old San Juan.
La atardecer por la bahía de San Juan.

Above (right): A building in Old San Juan.
Un edificio en el Viejo San Juan.

muchos se quisieron ir, pero los amenazaban con penas severas.

Casa Blanca, la residencia del gobernador, era de piedra y mampostería, a diferencia de las casas de madera de la mayoría de los colonizadores. Sin embargo, como defensa de San Juan no bastaba para espantar a los corsarios franceses o los piratas ingleses. Los bucaneros se apoderaban de las naves cargadas de riquezas rumbo a Europa y las que llegaban como suministros y mercancías de España.

El primer elemento del sistema de defensa fue La Fortaleza, cuyo aspecto era más de un castillo medieval que de un fuerte. Debido a su ubicación dentro de la bahía y no a su entrada, los enemigos de los españoles creían que el poblado estaba desprotegido. En 1539 se comenzó la construcción de San Felipe del Morro en la loma a la entrada de la bahía.

Los ataques continuaban y en las próximas décadas los españoles se vieron obligados a fortificar

be fortified. San Juan became one of the few cities in America completely surrounded by walls. By 1630 the imposing sandstone walls as well as San Cristóbal fort on the northeast sector of the city were being built. El Morro, rising 140 feet above the sea, defended the city at the entrance to San Juan Bay. San Cristóbal, to the east, guarded it from the land. Building the forts was a gigantic project, and was not completed until the early 1790s.

El Morro is very imposing, set on a crag overlooking the crashing waves of the Atlantic. There are many tales and legends about the forts, and some claim that certain sentry boxes, the *garitas*, are haunted. It is not hard to imagine young, lonely soldiers, far from home, scared as they take their night watch in one of the boxes nearest the roaring sea. The farthest sentry box was eventually closed, as several soldiers were washed away during rough night storms. "The evil one from the sea" brought terror into many hearts, and none wanted to go down there for the dreaded watch duty.

Sanjuaneros say ghosts wander the tunnels of El Morro. Over the years, many people were imprisoned in its dark and damp dungeons. One of the early Puerto Rican patriots, Buenaventura Quiñones, was found hung by a sheet in his cell.

Above: San Justo Street in Old San Juan.
La Calle de San Justo en El Viejo San Juan.

Top: The Plaza de Armas of San Cristóbal and the Chapel of Santa Barbara on the right.
La Plaza de Armas de San Cristóbal y la Capilla de Santa Bárbara a la derecha.

el puerto. Cuando Sir Francis Drake atacó a la isla en 1595 El Morro tenía 32 cañones. Después de una batalla con grandes bajas, Drake fue derrotado. Sin embargo, tres años después el Conde de Cumberland conquistó a San Juan, entrando por tierra. Después de seis semanas, tuvo que retirarse al morir muchos de sus soldados de disentería. Al regresar los españoles, se fortificó la ciudad completa, rodeándose la ciudad de murallas altas. Se construyó el fuerte San Cristóbal para proteger a la ciudad en contra de ataques por tierra. Este gran proyecto de construcción se vino a completar en la década de 1790.

Hay muchas leyendas acerca de los fuertes. Los sanjuaneros dicen haber visto fantasmas en las garitas y los túneles. Fueron muchos los presos en las mazmorras de El Morro; algunos murieron ahí. Un patriota puertorriqueño, Buenaventura Quiñones fue encontrado ahorcado en una sábana. ¿Suicidio? ¿Accidente? No se sabe, pero muchos dicen que divaga por los pasillos. El punto más alto de la ciudad es una loma detrás de El Morro. Ahí estuvo la Ermita de Santa Bárbara, que gozaba de una vista del Atlántico hacia el norte y de la bahía hacia el sur. Cuando se divisaba una nave en el horizonte, los monjes repicaban

Suicide or murder? To this day the question hasn't been answered, and some claim to have seen his ghost.

The highest point in the city was not, as many think, El Morro, but the hermitage on the hill behind it. La Hermita de Santa Barbara boasted a panoramic view of the Atlantic to the north and east and of the tranquil bay to the south. When a ship was spotted the monks sounded bells and people yelled, *"Vela! Vela!"* ("Sail! Sail!"). Until the flag designating country of origin came into view, the townspeople nervously prepared for attack.

Building the two forts cost a great deal of time, money, and manpower. Puerto Rico was the crossroads of America for Spain as well as her enemies. The forts of San Juan were not only to protect Puerto Rico but also to secure Spain's empire. With its safe harbor, San Juan served as a port of entry and a place of acclimatization for people and plants coming from Spain. As a naval station and base depot, it served as a stimulus to progress in industry, agriculture, and the arts.

The fort of San Cristóbal protected the most exposed part of San Juan. It is a spectacular construction, and, unlike at El Morro, the terrain had to be adapted to the fortification. Sandstone was cut from the hillside and a large cavity, the great moat, was built to hide the fort. It is 120 feet from the moat to *el macho* at the top of the fort.

This work required a great deal of manpower. During the peak of construction, more than 400 laborers worked on the forts and walls. Much of the labor gang consisted of convicts, slaves, and soldiers, as well as civilians. Many of the people set up camps around the forts, in front of and behind the city walls.

By the time the forts and walls were completed, the entire city was surrounded, and access was possible only through the gates. The

Above: A sentry box outside the main walls of San Cristóbal looking north over the Atlantic Ocean.
Una garita fuera de las murallas principales de San Cristóbal mirando norte hacia el Mar Atlántico.

Right: San José Plaza and the statue of Ponce de León. The white building is the San José Church, the second-oldest church in the Western Hemisphere.
La Plaza de San José y la estatua de Ponce de León. El edificio blanco es la Iglesia de San José, la segunda más antigua del hemisferio occidental.

las campanas; la gente gritaba ¡Vela! ¡Vela! Hasta que se podía identificar su nacionalidad el pueblo se preparaba para un posible ataque

La construcción de los fuertes tomó tiempo, dinero y esfuerzo. Aunque Puerto Rico se consideraba una isla pobre, era un punto clave para las Américas. Los fuertes de San Juan protegían no solo a Puerto Rico sino a la flota española. Con su puerto asegurado, San Juan era un lugar para que la gente y sus plantas y sus animales se aclimataran, además de ser un punto de aprovisionamiento y comercio, lo cual servía de estímulo a la industria, la agricultura y las artes.

El fuerte San Cristóbal protegía la parte más expuesta de San Juan. Es una construcción espectacular, y a diferencia de El Morro, hubo que adaptar el terreno a la fortificación. Se sacó piedra arenisca del monte, y se construyó un gran foso seco para ocultar el fuerte. Hay una distancia de 120 pies entre el fondo del foso a lo que se llama "el macho", el punto más alto del fuerte.

Se ocuparon muchos hombres en las obras: en el punto de mayor auge en la construcción había más de 400 obreros. Muchos de éstos eran presos, esclavos y militares, además de civiles, teniendo por vivienda tiendas de campaña que montaban dentro y fuera de las murallas.

Al terminarse la construcción de los fuertes y las murallas, se había rodeado la ciudad y se podía entrar únicamente por sus tres puertas: la Puerta de San Juan, que existe hoy día, la puerta de San Justo, al final de la calle de San Justo, que daba al puerto, y la Puerta de Santiago, más abajo del Fuerte San Cristóbal.

Varias batallas se libraron en contra de las agresivas fuerzas inglesas y holandesas. El último de los ataques fue el que comandó Sir Ralph Abercromby en 1797. Aunque su flota era de 68 naves y eran 7000 hombres, a la postre se tuvo que retirar, declarando que el puerto

three main entrances to San Juan were the San Juan Gate, which exists today, the San Justo Gate at the end of San Justo Street and exiting from the city to the port, and Santiago Gate, below San Cristóbal Fort. Each gate had its own function. Ships on their way to the port stopped first at the gate of San Juan. The San Justo Gate provided access to the city from the docks. And Santiago Gate, to the east, provided access from the rest of the island.

Several battles were waged against the aggressive British and Dutch forces. The last attack on San Juan was by Sir Ralph Abercromby in 1797, but the forts withstood his armada of 68 ships containing 600 guns and 7,000 troops. Eventually he retreated, admitting that the San Juan defenses were "both by Nature and Art, very strong."

After the Declaration of Independence in what was to become the United States, and the collapse of the Spanish empire, San Juan was no longer as important as a defense to the gateway of the Caribbean.

The conditions of the city rapidly deteriorated. The population swelled from 7,000 military and civilians to over 24,000 people. Overcrowded, there were only 926 buildings to house all of these residents. The city grew within its walls. Plazas were built, and used daily by the populace. Little by little, the streets were paved with blue slag bricks from Europe, more and more commerce came through the city, and homeowners began to build second floors to their homes, or divide them into multi-roomed dwellings centered on interior courtyards.

In the 19th century, agriculture in Puerto Rico expanded and the export of coffee, sugar, and tobacco brought the city economic growth.

The buildings in the north sector of the city, Santa Barbara, just below the forts and the city walls, were dedicated to institutional functions.

Above: San Cristóbal from the air looking south.
San Cristóbal del aire mirando hacia el sur.

de San Juan era "por Naturaleza y por Arte" demasiado fuerte para él.

Después de la Declaración de Independencia de los Estados Unidos y el colapso del imperio español, San Juan perdió su importancia como Llave de las Indias para los españoles.

Las condiciones de vida se hacían más difíciles, aumentando la población de 7000 a 24,000 habitantes aunque había solamente 926 edificios en donde acomodarlos. La ciudad crecía hacía adentro, con la construcción de nuevas plazas y la pavimentación de sus calles con adoquines. Sin embargo, la actividad comercial también aumentaba y se construían segundas plantas en las casas o se dividían para acomodar a más de una familia. En el siglo XIX, la agricultura experimentó un auge, y las exportaciones de café, azúcar y tabaco trajeron consigo el crecimiento económico.

La parte norte de la ciudad, el sector Santa Bárbara, estaba ocupada por los edificios del gobierno: los cuarteles de Ballajá, el manicomio, el corral de caballos y mulas, que suplía el mercado, y la plaza de mercado, construida en 1855. Esta plaza era un centro importante en la vida sanjuanera. Funcionaba de día y de noche. Ahí se compraba carbón para los fogones, hamacas, leche, viandas y frutas que traían los jíbaros del campo; se escuchaba el alboroto de las gallinas y los gallos; se ofrecía la quincallería en quioscos que rodeaban una plaza interior bastante grande. Casi todos los sanjuaneros, no importa su clase social, iban a la plaza por lo menos una vez al día. Ahí se enteraban de las noticias y de los chismes del día. En los cafetines se reunían los políticos y los artistas en sus tertulias. Hoy día es el Museo de Arte e Historia de San Juan.

El hacinamiento en la ciudad llegó a tal punto que en 1897 se derrumbó la Puerta de Santiago. Al cabo del tiempo fueron derribaras gran parte de las murallas y la Puerta de San Justo. El año siguiente, 1898, las tropas del ejército de Estados Unidos

The high ground symbolically was dedicated to centers of power. The army barracks of Ballajá, the biggest ever built by Spain, as well as an insane asylum, a corral for the horses and mules which served the marketplace, and the marketplace itself were built there.

The market, or *plaza de mercado*, wove an important fiber in the life of San Juan. Finished in 1855, it had many small businesses and kiosks set up around its large interior patio. *Campesinos* (country farmers) arrived early in the morning, rambling up the streets on oxen- or horse-driven carts filled with all kinds of products: fruits, vegetables, legumes, milk, boxes of squawking poultry, hammocks, stuffing for pillows, gourds, and tropical wood charcoal for the *fogones*, or open stoves. Most Sanjuaneros, no matter what their social class, went to the market at least once a day. It was the place where news and gossip were exchanged. Open 24 hours, its coffee stands were an

Above: Shops, storage and kitchen areas in El Morro's lower patio.
Talleres, almacenaje, y áreas de cocina en el patio bajo de El Morro.

Facing page (top): The lower patio or Level III of El Morro. The enlisted men of the fort lived here. Kitchens, latrines and a blacksmith shop surrounded the barracks area.
El patio inferior, Nivel III de El Morro. La guarnición vivía aquí. Las cocinas, letrinas y una herrería rodeaban el cuartel.

Left: El Morro from Ballajá plaza.
El Morro desde la Plaza de Ballajá.

desembarcaron en Puerto Rico, entrando por Guánica al suroeste de la isla. La isla fue cedida al gobierno de Estados Unidos en octubre de ese año.

Al pasar los años, muchos puertorriqueños emigraron a Estados Unidos y San Juan se fue despoblando. Hoy día, aproximadamente 9000 personas viven en lo que se conoce como el Viejo San Juan. Los sanjuaneros siempre han sido participantes activos en el destino de su ciudad: aprobaron que se derribara parte de las murallas y tomaron parte activa en la creación de sus plazas. Los residentes actuales tienen una Asociación de Residentes y juntos con el Instituto de Cultura, la Oficina de Preservación Histórica y el Servicio Nacional de Parques, luchan por restaurar y conservar a la ciudad. Los asuntos como el cierre de las calles al tránsito de vehículos de motor, los permisos para cierto tipo de negocio, y la reglamentación de las fiestas, se han convertido en temas de gran emotividad para ellos.

Antes de la fundación del Instituto de Cultura,

important gathering spot for the many political leaders and artists of the city. Today it is the Museo de Arte e Historia de San Juan.

By 1897 the city was bursting at its seams. With the urging of its citizens and with much fanfare, the Santiago Gate, the main entranceway to the city, was razed in a great blast. Eventually, the entire southeastern section of the wall, past the San Justo Gate, was destroyed to accommodate expansion.

Puerto Rico was invaded by the U.S. Army in July, 1898, not in San Juan but in Guánica on the southwest coast. The island was ceded to the United States in October, 1898.

People began to migrate to the United States, and little by little the population decreased. Today there are about 9,000 residents in the Old City.

San Juan's residents have always taken a strong role in approving or disapproving certain constructions. Not only did they approve leveling the walls to allow greater access to and from the city but they also were instrumental in the design and use of the plazas.

Today the Old San Juan Resident Association as well as the Institute of Culture, the State Historic Preservation Office, and the National Park Service fight to restore and preserve the city. Issues such as closing streets to traffic, permits for certain businesses, and regulations regarding festivities have often become emotional issues for residents of San Juan concerned with saving the city from further degradation.

Until the founding of the Puerto Rican Institute of Culture, many buildings of the Old City fell into disrepair. During the 1960s the city came to harbor a variety of night life, both Bohemian and what could be called shady. There were many well-known bordellos, as well as hidden-away bars and clubs. Puerto Rico attracted many night club entertainers and people looking for sun and fun, and this was reflected in many after-hours

The Devil's Sentry Box, the north walls of San Cristóbal and the Atlantic coast of Puerto Rico.

La Garita del Diablo, las murallas nortes de San
Cristóbal y la costa Atlántica de Puerto Rico.

spots. However, in recent decades Old San Juan became more and more residential as the character of tourism changed. Many buildings and homes have been restored, under the watchful guidelines of the Institute of Culture, and the city is gradually becoming gentrified. However, many different socio-economic classes and political/artistic ideas still mingle on its narrow streets.

Today Old San Juan is still a living, vibrant city. Its residents, merchants, and visitors breathe the cool damp air of the centuries as they enter buildings and mingle with the present and the past. Old San Juan is more than history, more than interior patios behind thick wooden doors, more than underground cisterns converted to wine cellars, ancient cannon facing the sea, and the faint echo of other times. Old San Juan is beloved for its kaleidoscope of people. It is the old man selling lottery tickets in front of the Post Office. It is Aladino, the shoe repair man; it is the painters, sculptors, and graphic artists in their studios; it is the domino players in Salvador Brau Plaza; it is the cat lady, leaving food for hundreds of feline residents; it is the children, feeding pigeons in the park and flying their *chiringas* (kites) on the grounds of El Morro; it is lovers, strolling through the city gate and to El Paseo de la Princesa; it is the fishermen dropping a line off the pier. It is masons and craftsmen lovingly restoring their heritage. Old San Juan is the past, the present and the future of Puerto Rico. It is its most precious museum.

Above: Flowers and the Aduana, the custom house on the bay in Old San Juan.
Flores y la Aduana en la bahía del Viejo San Juan.

muchos edificios del Viejo San Juan habían sido abandonados. Durante la década de 1960 la ciudad se conocía por su vida nocturna, pero recientemente se ha ido restaurando. Sin embargo, no ha perdido la mezcla de clases sociales que lo caracteriza y todavía se escuchan en sus estrechas calles las animadas conversaciones entre personajes de la vida política, artística y cultural.

El Viejo San Juan de hoy es una ciudad viviente, despierta. Sus residentes, comerciantes y visitantes pueden sentir el aliento de los siglos al entrar en los edificios antiguos. Pero San Juan es algo más que historia; algo más que los zaguanes y los patios interiores; algo más que las cisternas convertidas en cavas de vinos; y algo más que los cañones de cara al mar con su evocación de los tiempos de antaño. El Viejo San Juan es un lugar entrañable por su gente: el vendedor de lotería frente al Correo; Aladino el zapatero; los pintores, escultores y artistas gráficos; los jugadores de dominó de la Plaza de la Barandilla; la doña que alimenta a la población felina de la ciudad; los niños tirándole maíz a las palomas o volando chiringa en El Morro; los novios en el Paseo de la Princesa; los pescadores en el muelle; los albañiles y artesanos que se esfuerzan por conservar su patrimonio. El Viejo San Juan es el pasado, el presente y el futuro de Puerto Rico. Es su museo más preciado.

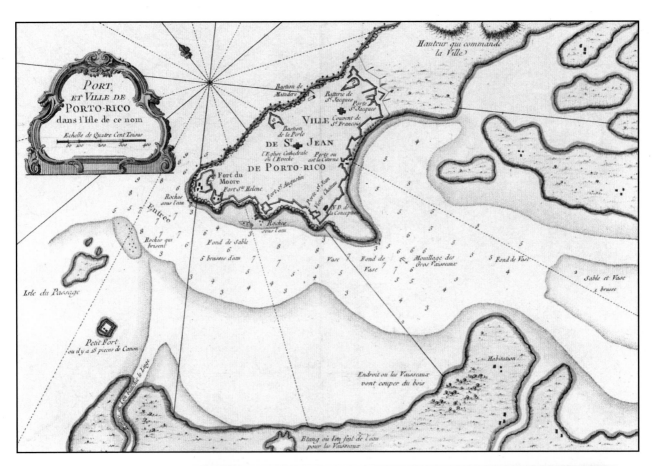

Above: Map made in 1671.
Carta del 1671.

Right: Ammunition in El Morro's magazine room.
Depósito de municiones en El Morro.

A passageway to troop quarters in El Morro.
Un pasillo hacia los cuarteles dentro de El Morro.

Above: Fortaleza Street and La Fortaleza, the Governor's Mansion.
Calle de La Fortaleza y La Fortaleza, Mansión del Gobernador.

Facing page (top left): Pigeon houses in Pigeon Park.
Casetas de palomas en el Parque de las Palomas.

Small business in Old San Juan.
Negocio pequeño en el Viejo San Juan.

Above: Buildings in Old San Juan.
Edicificos del Viejo San Juan.

El Morro's main battery level. The greatest concentration of cannons was placed in this area.
El nivel principal de El Morro con la mayor concentración de emplazamientos.

El Morro's chapel.
La capilla de El Morro.

Above: From the west end of San Cristóbal looking along Norzagaray Street toward El Morro. Segments of the Old City wall are visible.
Del oeste de San Cristóbal mirando por la Calle Norzagaray hasta El Morro. Se ven segmentos de las murallas.

Above (right): An original mesh shirt made in the 1500s. San Cristóbal.
Armadura de malla del siglo XVI.

Facing page (top left): The original Santa Barbara statue carved in the 1600s. Santa Barbara was the patron saint of artillery men. San Cristóbal.
La estatua original de Santa Bárbara data del siglo XVII. Santa Bárbara es la santa patrona de los artilleros.

Facing page (bottom): A cannon on the North Battery of San Cristóbal.
Un cañon en la batería del norte de San Cristóbal.

Above: Monjas Street in Old San Juan.
Caleta de las Monjas en el Viejo San Juan.

Left: San Juan Gate, the west wall and La Fortaleza, the oldest governor's mansion still used as such in the Western Hemisphere. La Fortaleza is part of Old San Juan's World Heritage Site.
La Puerta de San Juan, la muralla al oeste y La Fortaleza, la residencia más antigua de un gobernante en el hemisferio occidental. La Fortaleza pertenece al Sitio de Patrimonio Mundial de San Juan.

Colorful bougainvillea bloom in Old San Juan.
Trinitarias en el Viejo San Juan.

San José Church.
La Iglesia de San José.

Above: From San Cristóbal fortifications looking at the Atlantic Ocean.
Del fuerte de San Cristóbal mirando hacia el Mar Atlántico.

Facing page: An interior walkway leading to three of the main tunnels in San Cristóbal.
Pasillo interior que lleva a los tres túneles principales de San Cristóbal.

The promenade along the Old City wall. The wall was completed in the 1700s. It's made of sandstone blocks up to 20 feet thick; the walls surrounded the entire colonial city.

El paseo por las murallas de la ciudad, completadas en el siglo XVIII. Las murallas que rodeaban toda la ciudad, son de piedra arenisca y a veces alcanzan un grosor de 20 pies.

Left: Decorative street sign in Old San Juan.
Letrero decorativo de una calle en el Viejo San Juan.

Below: Paseo de la Princesa and la Princesa, a former jail and now the main office of the Puerto Rican Tourism Company.
Paseo de la Princesa y la Princesa, antes una prisión y ahora la oficina principal de la Compañía de Turismo de Puerto Rico.

Right: Some of El Morro's cannon emplacements.
Algunos de los emplazamientos de los cañones de El Morro.

Below: From El Morro's entry looking toward the former soldiers' barracks on the left and the harbor on the right.
Desde la entrada de El Morro mirando hacia los cuarteles militares antiguos a la izquierda y el puerto a la derecha.

El Morro's cannon emplacements on Level IV.
Los emplazamientos de los cañones de El Morro en el Nivel IV.

Right: Stylish hats on display in Old San Juan.
Sombreros en exhibición en el Viejo San
Juan.

The Plaza de Armas and the former Provincial Delegation Building, now Puerto Rico's State Department.
La Plaza de Armas y el Departamento de Estado.

From the upper reaches of San Cristóbal looking toward Columbus Plaza and part of Old San Juan.
En la parte superior de San Cristóbal mirando hacia la Plaza Colón y parte del Viejo San Juan.

Right: Cruz Street in Old San Juan.
Calle de la Cruz en el Viejo San Juan.

The Christ Chapel and the silver altar.
La Capilla de Cristo y su altar de plata.

Above (left): One of six gates to Old San Juan, which for centuries were closed at sundown to protect the city.
Una de las seis puertas del Viejo San Juan. Durante siglos se cerraban al atardecer para proteger a la ciudad.

Top: Plaza de la Rogativa.

Fire boat by San Juan Bay.
Barco de bomberos en la bahía de San Juan.

Top: The capitol building of Puerto Rico.
El Capitolio de Puerto Rico.

Cristo Street in Old San Juan.
Calle del Cristo en el Viejo San Juan.

Above: The corner of Calle del Cristo and San Sebastian.
Esquina de la Calle del Cristo y la Calle de San Sebastián.

Above: One of many tunnels and passageways inside San Cristóbal.
Uno de los numerosos túneles y pasadizos dentro de San Cristóbal.

Right: The dungeon of San Cristóbal.
El calabozo de San Cristóbal.

Above: Early-day prison graffiti in the San Cristóbal dungeon.
Escritos de los presos en el calabozo de San Cristóbal.

Top: One of the last discovered tunnel areas in El Morro. The enlisted men
of the fort lived here. Kitchens, latrines and a blacksmith shop surrounded
the barracks area.
Uno de los túneles descubiertos recientemente en El Morro. Esta es
la parte más antigua del fuerte.

The western sector of Old San Juan and the San Juan Bay from the air.

Desde el aire el sector oeste del Viejo San Juan y el Morro.

Sol Street in Old San Juan.
Calle del Sol en el Viejo San Juan.

San Juan Cathedral. Cathedral Metropolitana de San Juan Bautista. The church was built in 1540 and refurbished in the early 1800s.
Catedral de San Juan. Catedral Metropolitana de San Juan Bautista. Construida en 1540 y restaurada a principios del siglo XIX.

Inside the San Juan Cathedral.
Dentro de la Catedral de San Juan.

Right: Main entry to El Morro.
Entrada principal de El Morro.

Below: The upper level of El Morro.
This area was designed to protect
against land attacks and faces the
city, rather than the sea.
El nivel superior de El Morro.
Esta área fue diseñada para
proteger el fuerte contra ataques
desde tierra y tiene una vista
hacia la ciudad en vez de hacia el
mar.

Vaulted artillery ramp leading from Level V down to the lower parts of El Morro.
Rampa abovedada de artillería desde el Nivel V hasta las partes inferiores de El Morro.

Above: Sunset on the Paseo de la Princesa.
Atardecer en el Paseo de la Princesa.

Right: The bronze sculpture in this fountain on the Paseo de la Princesa symbolizes the island's cultural roots.
La escultura de bronce de esta fuente en el Paseo de la Princesa ilustra las raíces culturales de la Isla.

San Cristóbal barracks. Overall the barracks could house 212 soldiers.
El Cuartel de San Cristóbal que se podía acomadar a 212 soldados.

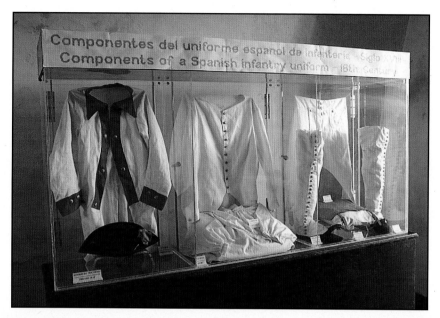

Above: The Chapel of Santa Barbara in San Cristóbal with a replica of the original statue.
La Capilla de Santa Bárbara en San Cristóbal con una réplica de la estatua original.

Top: An 18th century Spanish infantry uniform.
Uniforme de infantería español, siglo XVIII.

Above: Main artillery ramp to Ochoa Bastion.
La rampa principal de artillería en dirección
hacia el Bastión Ochoa.

Top: An original Spanish cannon in San Cristóbal.
Un cañon original español en San Cristóbal.

Facing page: North walls of El Morro.
Murallas del norte de El Morro.

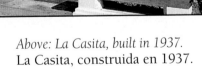

Above: La Casita, built in 1937.
La Casita, construida en 1937.

Top: Pigeon Park.
Parque de las Palomas.

Garden at Casa Blanca.
Jardines de Casa Blanca.

Cristo Street in Old San Juan.
Calle del Cristo en el Viejo San Juan.

Right: San Juan Cemetery.
Cementerio de San Juan.

Below: Fort San Gerónimo—just to the east of Old San Juan.
El Fuerte San Gerónimo—al este del Viejo San Juan.

The Alcaldía or City Hall completed in 1789 still serves as Old San Juan's City Hall.
La Alcaldía completada en el 1789 todavia funciona como tal.

A cruise ship in San Juan Bay.
Crucero en la bahía de San Juan.

Above: Atlantic shoreline near San Cristóbal.
La costa del Atlántico cerca de San Cristóbal.

Right: From within El Morro looking east toward San Cristóbal.
Mirando desde adentro de El Morro hacia San Cristóbal al este.

El Morro's main plaza. This was the focal point for the troops that manned the fort. Officers' quarters and cannon-firing positions surround the plaza as well as storerooms for food and ammunition. The lighthouse in this photo was built by United States forces in 1908.

La plaza principal de El Morro, punto de concentración para la guarnición. Los cuarteles de los oficiales y los emplazamientos rodean la plaza, además de los almacenes de comestibles y los polvorines. El faro en esta fotografía fue construido por los EE.UU. en 1908.

An approximate replica of the Santa Maria used by Columbus; no actual prints or drawings of the ship are known to have survived. El Morro.

Réplica aproximada de la Santa María, nave de Cristóbal Colón. No tenemos plano ni dibujo de esta nave.

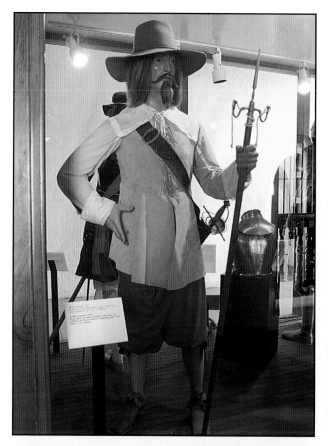

Above: An artillery officer of the 1741 Fixed Regiment of Puerto Rico. Troops from this regiment defended the city against the British attack in 1797. El Morro.
Oficial de artillería del Regimiento Fijo de Puerto Rico en 1741. Los artilleros de este regimiento defendieron la ciudad contra los ingleses en 1797.

Top (left): A 1625 Spanish gunner. El Morro.
Artillero español de 1625. El Morro.

Left: An 1898 artillery man. This was the garrison uniform used by the Spanish in Puerto Rico and Cuba during the Spanish American War. El Morro.
Artillero de 1898. Este fue el uniforme de guarnición usado por los españoles en Puerto Rico y en Cuba durante la Guerra Hispanoamericana.

The north walls and the Devil's Sentry Box of San Cristóbal looking west across La Perla to El Morro.
Las murallas del norte y la Garita del Diablo de San Cristóbal mirando hacia oeste y por encima de La Perla hasta El Morro.

Left: From San Cristóbal looking at San Juan Bay.
De San Cristóbal mirando hacia la Bahía de San Juan.

Below: The outworks of San Cristóbal—the gun placement in the center of the photo was used during World War II.
La obra exterior de San Cristóbal. El emplazamiento en el centro de la fotografía se usó en la Segunda Guerra Mundial.

Inside San Juan Cathedral.
Interior de la Catedral de San Juan.

Left: A jewelry display in Old San Juan.
Una exhibición de joyería en el Viejo San Juan.

Bottom: Tapia Theater built in the 19th century.
El Teatro Tapia, construido durante el siglo XIX.

Above: El Convento—a former convent of the Carmelite nuns, now a hotel in Old San Juan.
El Convento. Antiguo convento de las monjas Carmelitas, ahora un hotel.

Left: Hand-painted tiles decorate an Old San Juan street sign.
Losetas pintadas a mano decoran un letrero en el Viejo San Juan.

Above: The former Asilo de Beneficencia or home for the poor. Built in the 1840s.
El antiguo Asilo de Beneficencia, construido en la década de 1840.

The western sector of Old San Juan and El Morro from the air.

Desde el aire el sector oeste del Viejo San Juan y El Morro.

Above: Plaza del Quinto Centenario.
This plaza symbolizes five centuries of
Puerto Rican history.
Plaza del Quinto Centenario. Esta
plaza simbolíza los 5 siglos de la
historia puertorriqueña.

Right: The Casa San José Hotel and
San José Street in Old San Juan.
El Hotel Casa San José y la Calle de
San José en el Viejo San Juan.

Ballajá plaza and the Ballajá barracks, once home to Spanish troops and their families.
La plaza de Ballajá y los cuarteles de Ballajá, hospedaje de soldados españoles y sus familias.

San Cristóbal from the air looking south.
San Cristóbal desde el aire mirando hacia el sur.

Above: The Plaza de Armas,
Chapel of Santa Barbara and
barracks of San Cristóbal.
La Plaza de Armas, la capilla
de Santa Bárbara y los
cuarteles de San Cristóbal.

Left: Castillo de San Cristóbal.

Rick and Susie Beaulaurier Graetz have combined their love of travel, things new, and photographic skills to produce three photographic books on Montana, U.S.A., and one on Wyoming, U.S.A. Their photography has appeared in works on the West Indies, Europe, and Asia. Susie is the editor of the highly successful *Montana Celebrity Cookbook*. Rick is the publisher of *Montana Magazine* and American & World Geographic Publishing, as well as being an adventurer, mountain climber, writer, and photographer. In addition to his frequent magazine and newspaper columns on travel and world geography, he has been the author and photographer for books on Vietnam, Cuba, and Montana's Bob Marshall Wilderness. His photography graces the pages of a book profiling Helena, Montana, his home of over 25 years.

Patricia L. Wilson, who holds a Ph.D. in art education, is the owner and chef of the world-renowned Bistro Gambaro in Old San Juan, Puerto Rico. Before becoming a "culinary specialist," Wilson was a professor and research writer. The decor of the famous restaurant shows her to be an active member of a thriving art community. Since 1989, her show "What's Cooking With Patricia?" has aired twice a day on WOSO Radio, San Juan; her "What's Cooking…Saturday Edition" is a one-hour listener participation program. Her popular newspaper column, "From Soup to Salsa," appears each Wednesday in the *San Juan Star.*

If you would like to purchase additional copies of this book, check with your local bookstore or call American & World Geographic Publishing at 800-654-1105 or 406-443-2842, Monday through Friday, 8:00 A.M. to 5:00 P.M. Mountain Time, U.S.A.

Para comprar copias adicionales de este libro los puede pedir en su librería local o llamar a America & World Geographic Publishing al teléfono (800) 654-1105 o al (406) 443-2842, de lunes a viernes 8:00 A.M. hasta el 5:00 P.M. hora de Montana, E.U.